Half an Idea

A Comedy

Bob Larbey

A SAMUEL FRENCH ACTING EDITION

SAMUEL FRENCH

FOUNDED 1830

SAMUELFRENCH-LONDON.CO.UK
SAMUELFRENCH.COM

ISBN 978-0-573-12132-6

www.samuelfrench-london.co.uk

www.samuelfrench.com

FOR AMATEUR PRODUCTION ENQUIRIES

UNITED KINGDOM AND WORLD
EXCLUDING NORTH AMERICA
plays@SamuelFrench-London.co.uk

020 7255 4302/01

Each title is subject to availability from Samuel French,

depending upon country of performance.

CHARACTERS

Writer
Pauline
Mr Moore
Mrs Moore
Mrs Hurst
Catherine
Tamsin
Ted
Carol
Alice
Mr Dicks
Mrs Dicks
Mrs Cohen
Mr Wilson
Mrs Wilson
Madge
Mr Stiles
Stage Manager
Mr Charlton
Mrs Charlton
Mrs Peters
Carla
Mrs Banks
Cyril
Jackie
Edie
Vicar

The locations are: before the Curtains; in the living-rooms of a middle-class and a working-class home; in the Writer's home

Time: the present

Other plays by Bob Larbey published by
Samuel French Ltd:

Building Blocks

A Small Affair

A Small Affair may be presented as a double bill with
Half An Idea, using many of the same cast, to create a full
evening's entertainment. Performance fees for the double
bill will be given on application to Samuel French Ltd.

HALF AN IDEA

Front of CURTAIN L *are a desk and a chair. On the desk is a typewriter and a nearly-completed manuscript. By the side of the desk is a waste-paper basket with several pieces of screwed-up paper in it*

Writer is sitting at the desk. He strikes the last few keys with a sense of triumph

Writer Curtain!

The CURTAIN *opens*

No.

The CURTAIN *closes. Writer makes a few more keystrokes*

That's better. "The Curtain Falls!"

Stage Manager enters R. She looks at the CURTAIN *in bewilderment*

During the following exchanges, Stage Manager talks to Writer, but Writer talks to himself

Stage Manager It can't fall at all!
Writer No. Perhaps just "Curtain" is better.

Stage Manager dashes off

The CURTAIN *opens*

Stage Manager appears, breathing heavily

Stage Manager Just curtain?
Writer Yes. Just—just wonderfully, finally, brilliantly, triumphantly— "Curtain!"

Stage Manager Right!

Stage Manager exits

The CURTAIN *closes*

Writer (*shouting*) I've finished!

His wife, Pauline, enters

Pauline Shh! You'll wake the children.
Writer (*whispering*) I've finished.
Pauline I'm glad. I'm proud. Your first play. What's it about?
Writer Life!
Pauline Big subject.
Writer Why start with a little one? Actually, it's a rage *against* life.
Pauline It's not a comedy, then?
Writer Of course it's not a comedy! It's angry. John Osborne angry? This would make him look just very slightly annoyed.
Pauline May I read it?
Writer Of course. (*He gets up, giving Pauline his chair*)

As she begins to read, he hovers nervously

Pauline Act One. Scene One. The curtain rises.

Stage Manager enters

Stage Manager How many more times do I have to tell you?
Writer No. I've taken against curtains rising. The first thing you see that way is a lot of feet.
Stage Manager Exactly.
Writer And let's face it, feet are not that attractive. No—substitute— "The Curtains open".
Pauline Right. "The Curtains open!"

Stage Manager exits

The Lights on Writer and Pauline fade down

The CURTAIN *opens*

The set is a middle-class living-room

Mrs Charlton enters R. *She is dressed for a wedding*

Mrs Charlton Bring her through, Giles! Bring her through.

Mr Charlton (*off*) I'm trying to bring her through! She keeps leaning against the wall! Come on, Melissa, there's a good girl. That's it.

Mr Charlton enters R. *He is also dressed for a wedding. He supports Mrs Moore, the bride's mother. She seems near to collapse and her hat has fallen over one eye*

Mrs Moore I want to die! I want to die!

Mrs Charlton No, you don't. There's no point to that. Sit her down, Giles, do!

Mr Charlton lowers her on to the sofa

Mr Charlton There we are, old thing. (*His hands go to the buttons of Mrs Moore's blouse*)

She slaps his hands away

Mrs Moore Get away! Have you taken leave of your senses?

Mrs Charlton What on earth are you doing?

Mr Charlton I was loosening her clothing. Aren't you supposed to do that?

Mrs Charlton No, you are not!

Mr Charlton Should I stick her legs in the air?

Mrs Moore sits up quite straight

Mrs Moore You won't stick my legs anywhere!

Mr Charlton I was only trying to help. I read it somewhere—about sticking people's legs in the air.

Mrs Moore I'll be all right. It's the shock.

Mrs Charlton Of course it is. Giles, a brandy.

Mr Charlton Right.

Mrs Moore He should be horsewhipped.
Mrs Charlton Well, that's rather excessive. He *was* only trying to help.
Mrs Moore Not Giles. That thug who jilted my daughter!
Mrs Charlton (*with distaste*) Rick!
Mrs Moore I don't want to hear his name mentioned again!
Mrs Charlton No, of course not. How could any parent christen a child Rick with a surname like Dicks? I ask you, Rick Dicks.

Mr Charlton helps himself to brandy

Mrs Moore I had hoped against hope that it was an abbreviation for Richard. But no. At least my darling will never be known as Tamsin Dicks.

Mrs Charlton looks around to see her husband drinking

Mrs Charlton Giles! The brandy was for Melissa, not for you!
Mr Charlton Oh. Sorry. Quite.
Mrs Moore I don't want a brandy and I don't think I ever want to eat or drink again.

Mrs Charlton tuts sympathetically. Mr Charlton pours himself another brandy

Mr Charlton I'm not sure that's wise.

Mrs Hurst, the live-in housekeeper, enters L

Mrs Hurst I'm ever so sorry. I was having a lie-down with bits of cucumber over my eyes. I didn't expect anybody back for ages.
Mrs Moore How could you have, Mrs Hurst?
Mr Charlton Bits of cucumber?
Mrs Hurst I thought you'd all be at the reception.
Mrs Moore Hah!
Mrs Charlton There will be no reception, Mrs Hurst. There was no wedding.
Mrs Hurst Oh, I say! Didn't the vicar turn up?
Mrs Moore Tell her, Edwina.
Mrs Charlton The bridegroom didn't turn up.

Mrs Hurst Well! That's not very polite, is it?

Mrs Moore Not very polite? It's an act of crass, imbecilic, thoughtless, cruel and unforgivable behaviour!

Mrs Hurst Well, yes, that as well. Is it all right if I tidy my person?

Mrs Moore Yes, by all means, Mrs Hurst, do tidy your person.

Mrs Hurst Thank you.

Mrs Hurst moves to the exit L

Mr Charlton Bits of cucumber on the eyes, you said?

Mrs Hurst Slices, more accurately.

Mr Charlton Any reason, or was it just a whim?

Mrs Hurst Wrinkles.

Mr Charlton Wrinkles?

Mrs Hurst You can use tea-bags.

Mrs Hurst exits L

Mr Charlton Funny creatures, women.

Mrs Charlton Don't you dare say a word about women! It's a man who brought today to ruin.

Mrs Moore Rick Dicks! And I never want that name mentioned in this house again!

Mrs Peters enters R

Mrs Peters Rick Dicks is a swine! They've all gone home. Roger's not with me because Mrs Bullock's hip gave out, so he ran her back to Oxshott. I brought Catherine with me.

Mr Charlton Who's all gone home?

Mrs Peters The guests.

Mr Charlton Well, that's damned bad form.

Mrs Peters You can't have a reception, not without a——

Mrs Moore Bridegroom! You were going to say "Bridegroom", weren't you?

Mrs Peters "Couple", actually.

Catherine enters R. *She is a young bridesmaid*

Mrs Moore Catherine! What a disappointment for you.

Catherine No, I'm all right. I thought it was quite exciting really.
Mrs Moore Exciting?
Catherine Well, anyone can have a wedding which goes off normally, can't they? At least ours was different.
Mrs Moore *Different!* Edwina, talk to her!
Mrs Charlton Catherine, this should have been a day which your sister would never forget!
Catherine Well, she won't, will she?
Mrs Moore Go to your room!
Catherine Oh Mum, don't be prehistoric. Anyway, I think Tamsin's well out of it. I think Rick Dicks is a total nerd.

She exits into the kitchen

(*Off*) Hallo, Uncle Giles. Getting drunk again?
Mrs Charlton What is a nerd, actually?
Mrs Peters It's a little creature on children's television, isn't it? I think it's shaped like a potato.
Mrs Moore As long as it isn't obscene.
Mrs Charlton It sounded derogatory, that's the main thing.

Mrs Hurst enters L

Mrs Hurst Here we are. I'm more myself. Now, is there anything I can do, Mrs Moore?
Mrs Moore You can't rebuild a life!
Mrs Hurst I'd thought more of making a cup of tea, or something.
Mrs Moore Oh, I see. Yes, make a cup of tea, by all means, Mrs Hurst.

Mrs Hurst makes for the kitchen

Catherine enters, eating a yoghurt

Mrs Hurst Oh Catherine, don't you look sweet? You look like a little doll.
Catherine Thank you, Mrs Hurst.

Mrs Hurst exits

(*After Mrs Hurst has gone*) Sweet! I swear she thinks I'm Shirley Temple!

Mrs Peters She was a dear little girl.
Catherine I am not a little girl. I'm going up to change before you ask me to sing *On The Good Ship Lollipop.*

Catherine exits huffily

Mr Charlton If you ask me——
Mrs Charlton Nobody *is* asking you, Giles.
Mrs Moore This fiasco will be round the district like a bushfire, of course. I shall be tittered at in Tesco's.
Mrs Peters I'm sure you won't be blamed, Melissa.
Mrs Moore Of course I won't. But I will be ridiculed. "That's the woman whose daughter was jilted by Rick Dicks."
Mr Charlton Wouldn't some sort of cover story help?
Mrs Moore Like what?
Mr Charlton Well—um—let me see. We could always say he was abducted.
Mrs Charlton Abducted?
Mr Charlton Yes.
Mrs Charlton By whom?
Mr Charlton Well, I don't know—abductors of some sort.

The three women look at each other

After all, it does happen.
Mrs Peters Not around here, surely?
Mr Charlton Who's to say? Red Brigades and so on.
Mrs Charlton Who presumably release him in time to go to work on Monday?
Mr Charlton Ah. Amnesia!

Mrs Hurst comes in on this with a tray of tea-things

Mrs Hurst Would aspirins help, Mr Charlton?
Mr Charlton Aspirins?
Mrs Hurst For your amnesia. It's shooting pains down the back of the legs, isn't it?
Mrs Moore Just put the tea down, please, Mrs Hurst.
Mrs Hurst I was only trying to help.

Mrs Hurst goes into the kitchen

Mrs Moore I can't pour. I'm not up to it.
Mrs Peters Let me.
Mr Charlton Nobody thinks amnesia's a good idea, then?
Mrs Charlton Oh, do shut up, Giles!
Mr Charlton Well, really.

Mrs Hurst enters from the kitchen

Mrs Hurst Mrs Moore, I've just had a thought.
Mrs Moore Are you going to tell it to me?
Mrs Hurst Yes. How many will there be for tea?
Mrs Moore You've just made the tea!
Mrs Hurst No, I mean tea-tea. I mean, as you didn't have the reception, people will be hungry, won't they?

This makes them all think

Mrs Moore We didn't tell the catering people. There's food and drink there for one hundred and thirty-eight people.
Mr Charlton I'd better whiz round in the Range Rover.
Mrs Charlton With the amount of brandy you've drunk, you're not whizzing round anywhere.
Mrs Peters Look, I'd be glad to do it. I don't want to cry when your Tamsin arrives.

Carla, another guest, hurries in

Carla Your husband's here with Tamsin, Mrs Moore.
Mrs Peters I'll pop out the back way. I don't want to cry.

Mrs Peters exits via the kitchen

Mrs Hurst Have we decided about the number for tea?
Mrs Moore Not now, Mrs Hurst!

Mrs Hurst exits into the kitchen

Mrs Charlton What do we do, Melissa?

Carla Think of Tamsin.

Mrs Moore Yes, we don't cry. We must be brave and bright for my Tamsin.

Tamsin enters with her father

The Ladies try to look brave and bright for her. Mrs Moore immediately bursts into tears and rushes to her daughter

Oh, my baby! My poor, poor baby!

Tamsin comforts her

Tamsin It's all right, Mum. Don't cry.

Mr Moore Yes, come on, Melissa—buck up.

Mrs Moore In case you've forgotten, I've been humiliated!

Tamsin That's funny, I thought it was me.

Carla Yes, I thought that too.

Mr Moore Yes, come on, darling. This is not a time to think of oneself. (*Suddenly*) My God! I've paid for all that food and drink at the reception!

Mrs Hurst enters from the kitchen

Mr Charlton It's all right, Harry. The Peters woman has gone round there.

Mrs Hurst She hasn't, actually. She's just come back.

Mrs Peters enters from the kitchen

Mrs Peters I'd forgotten. I don't have a car because Roger's taken Mrs Bullock's hip home! (*She sees Tamsin*) Oh, Tamsin. (*She starts to cry*)

Tamsin (*comforting her*) There, there. Cheer up.

Mr Moore Well, somebody should get round there.

Mr Charlton I did offer.

Mrs Charlton Oh, look, I'll drive.

Mr Charlton We can save the booze at least.

Mr and Mrs Charlton, and Mrs Peters, exit through the kitchen. Mrs Hurst touches Tamsin's hand and follows them

Carla What are they going to do with the food? Try to eat it all themselves?

Mr Moore I think jokes are in rather bad taste at a time like this.

Tamsin Well, you do have to see the funny side, don't you?

Mrs Moore Darling, there *isn't* a funny side.

Tamsin Isn't there? All those hats—all those suits—all those cars fresh from the car wash—and all for nothing.

Mrs Moore Harry, she's hysterical.

Mr Moore No, not hysterical. Odd.

Tamsin Then I've always been odd, haven't I? I've never quite fitted your picture. Tamsin! I mean, who calls anybody Tamsin? That's starting life with an anvil round your neck.

Mrs Moore You *are* hysterical.

Tamsin No, Mum, I'm really, really not. I'm really not. (*She crosses towards the exit*)

Mrs Moore Where are you going?

Tamsin To change. I mean, this isn't the sort of thing you wear round the house, is it?

Carla I'll come with you.

Tamsin and Carla go to the exit L

Catherine enters, now dressed casually

Catherine (*passing Tamsin and Carla*) I suppose you'll want your room back.

Tamsin Catherine, you really must stop thinking of others all the time.

Catherine (*to Carla*) I bet you wish you had a sister like me.

Carla It's a cross I have to bear.

Tamsin and Carla exit

Catherine crosses R

Catherine See you, then.

Mrs Moore Where are you going?

Catherine Pictures.

Mrs Moore Catherine, is this really the time?

Catherine Yes. It starts in twenty minutes. Bye.

She exits R

Mrs Moore That's your daughter!
Mr Moore I'm painfully aware of that.
Mrs Moore Why didn't you stop her?
Mr Moore From doing what?
Mrs Moore Oh!

Mrs Hurst enters from the kitchen

Mrs Hurst Look, I'm sorry, but I'm still in a state of suspension.
Mrs Moore What *are* you talking about?
Mrs Hurst The question of eating. When, what and how many for.
Mrs Moore You're getting obsessive about this, aren't you?
Mrs Hurst An army marches on its stomach.
Mrs Moore We are not an army!
Mr Moore Look, Mrs Hurst, there's enough food for one hundred and thirty-eight people coming back from the reception. I don't think you have to worry about preparing food!
Mrs Hurst Very well. You'll be sick of prawn vol-au-vents by the end of the week, though.
Mrs Moore Will you just take the tea-things?

Mrs Hurst clears up the tea-things

Mrs Hurst You could always have a party and get rid of them in one go.

They look at her

No. Perhaps not.

Mrs Hurst exits into the kitchen with the tray

Mrs Moore takes her hat off, sighs and sits down

Mrs Moore What are we going to do, Harry?
Mr Moore There's some rugby on television.
Mrs Moore About the wedding!
Mr Moore There wasn't one.

Mrs Moore Oh, don't be pedantic! You know very well what I mean.

Mr Moore I wonder if I could write some of it off against tax? I could always call it a conference.

Mrs Moore I sometimes feel I'm talking to a total stranger. All you're thinking about is the expense. Your daughter and your wife have been shamed!

Mr Moore Well, I can hardly fight a duel, can I?

Mrs Moore Sue!

Mr Moore Your sister?

Mrs Moore No! Sue for breach of promise. Drag that Dicks creature through the courts!

Mr Moore Tamsin as well?

Mrs Moore I'm beginning to want not to live!

Mr Moore There is a bright side to all this.

Mrs Moore Have you taken leave of your senses?

Mr Moore No. We shall never have Rick Dicks as our son-in-law.

Mrs Moore There is that.

Mr Moore We shall never have to see his ghastly family again.

Mrs Moore There's that as well. I knew what they were like the minute I saw the gnomes in their front garden.

Mr Moore His father, you know, kept calling me "mate".

A ring at the doorbell

Mrs Hurst enters from the kitchen to answer it

Mrs Hurst I'll go. I don't think I can get one hundred and thirty-eight prawn vol-au-vents in the freezer, anyway, you know.

She exits R

Mrs Moore Their door-chimes play *Viva España.*

Mr Moore What really hurts is that he makes much more money than I do.

Mrs Hurst enters

Mrs Hurst It's some people called The Spangle Sisters.

The Spangle Sisters enter. They are a young singing duo—Ted and Carol

Ted Hi. We're The Spangle Sisters.
Mr Moore That's biologically impossible.
Ted Come again?
Mr Moore One of you is a man.
Ted Oh, that. That's all right. That's the gimmick.

Alice enters. She is the third Spangle Sister, not in the first flush of youth

Alice I've parked the van in your drive. Is that all right?
Mr Moore No, it's not all right! Who *are* you?

Carol prowls about the room

Alice I'm the third Spangle Sister.
Carol She's my mum.
Alice I'm the drummer.
Carol How are you off for plugs?
Mrs Moore Plugs?
Carol For the amps.
Mrs Moore I don't know what you're talking about.
Carol Amplifiers—for the guitars.
Alice And I'll need a hand with my drums.
Mrs Hurst I'll do that. You're not from round here, are you?
Alice No. I'm from Hampshire.
Mrs Hurst Oh, a lovely county. I'm from Somerset.
Alice Oh, that's a lovely county too.
Mrs Hurst How long have you been a drummer, then?
Alice Only two years.
Mrs Hurst It must be wonderful to be musical. I did try to learn the mouth-organ once, but——
Mrs Moore Mrs Hurst, please! Harry?
Mr Moore Yes. Now, look here, Mr Spangle——
Ted Ted.
Carol I'm Carol—no *e* on the end.
Alice And I'm Alice. That does have an *e* on the end.
Mr Moore Yes, yes. The fact is that we have no idea of what you're doing here.
Ted We're the entertainment.
Carol At the wedding reception.

Mrs Moore Does this look like a wedding reception? The wedding reception was cancelled!

Ted Well, that did become obvious when nobody turned up.

Mrs Moore Then why have you come here?

Carol Because we're professionals, that's why.

Alice Evenings and weekends. We work at the Co-Op during the day.

Ted The Co-Op is just a stepping stone.

Carol All right, semi-professionals. But the fact is, if we're paid for a gig, we *do* a gig.

Mrs Hurst That's very admirable. Would any of you care for a prawn vol-au-vent? I've got one hundred and thirty-eight coming.

Mrs Moore Mrs Hurst, please!

Mr Moore Now, see here! You're not doing a jig in my living-room.

Ted No, "Gig"—that's "Gig".

Mr Moore I don't care what it is, you're not doing it in my living-room! Who hired you in the first place?

Ted A Mr Rick Dicks.

Mrs Moore I might have known.

Mr Moore Then why not go to *his* house and annoy him?

Ted "Entertain" is the word.

Alice We've got lights as well.

Carol Yes. In any case, we did discuss that, but we decided the bride's house was more appropriate. After all, it is her day.

Mrs Moore Her day? She's been jilted!

Alice Oh, dear.

Mrs Hurst Terrible, isn't it?

Ted Then we might cheer her up.

Mr Moore Now, look, Mr Spangle——

Ted Ted.

Mr Moore Ted, then. Nothing is going to cheer this house up today, least of all The Spangle Sisters. I'd be most grateful if you would simply go.

Carol Back to Croydon?

Mr Moore If that's where you came from, yes.

Mrs Hurst I had an aunt in Croydon. She had no lobes to her ears.

Mrs Moore Mrs Hurst!

Ted Look, you are sure about this? You don't even want us to do a couple of standards?

Carol A bit of Motown?

Alice Heavy Metal?

Mr Moore Thank you, no.
Ted Right, then. Come on—back to Croydon.
Carol Back to being just Ted and Carol again.
Alice And Alice.
Carol And Alice, Mum. ·
Ted Well, then. Good-afternoon, everybody.

They turn to go

Oh. If the wedding should happen to get rearranged—our card. (*He hands over a card*)
Carol The phone number's Gran's. She does the bookings.
Alice She's our agent.
Ted But you'll have to speak up because she's a bit deaf.
Mrs Hurst I'll see you out.

Mrs Hurst and the Spangle Sisters exit

Mrs Moore The Spangle Sisters!
Mr Moore From Croydon.
Mrs Moore Our Tamsin could have married into a family who liked The Spangle Sisters!
Mr Moore But that's it! This isn't such a bad day after all. We need never have anything to do with the Dicks family again!

Mrs Hurst enters

Mrs Hurst Mr and Mrs Rick Dicks!

As Mr and Mrs Dicks enter, the atmosphere freezes

Mr Dicks Good-afternoon.
Mr Moore Good-afternoon.
Mrs Dicks Good-afternoon.
Mrs Moore Good-afternoon.
Mrs Hurst Well, I'll leave you all to chat.
Mr Dicks Well, this is a fine kettle of fish, isn't it?
Mrs Dicks A right pickle.
Mrs Moore Pickle or fish, this catastrophe is of your own making!

Mrs Dicks That's not fair. We didn't tell our Rick not to turn up.
Mr Dicks He thought of that all by himself.
Mr Moore Well, don't make it sound like a boast!
Mrs Moore My daughter is distraught!
Mrs Dicks She seemed to take it all very calmly to me.
Mrs Moore That's courage. That's breeding.
Mrs Dicks Implying we don't have any?
Mrs Moore You may draw your own conclusions.
Mrs Dicks I already have, you supercilious trout!
Mr Moore I'll thank you to withdraw that remark, madam!
Mr Dicks Don't you call my wife a madam!
Mrs Dicks You never thought my Rick was good enough for your daughter, did you?
Mrs Moore In a word, no.
Mr Dicks You kill me, you people!
Mr Moore Believe me, I'd quite like to.
Mr Dicks Oh, ha-ha! You swank about as though you own the world. You're all coffee mornings and double garages, you are.
Mrs Dicks *We've* got a treble garage.
Mr Dicks Exactly.
Mr Moore Which proves that you want something you can never have a bit of.
Mr Dicks Class? Is that what you were going to say?
Mr Moore Yes. Very well. Class.
Mrs Moore Game, set and match, I think.
Mrs Dicks Oh, do you? Well, let me tell you this. You've got about as much class as the bunion on my left foot!

The doorbell rings

Mrs Hurst enters from the kitchen to answer

Mrs Hurst I'll go!

She exits

Mr Moore Now, look here, we've gone off the point entirely. The point is that your son has betrayed our daughter. What the hell happened?
Mr Dicks We don't know. We haven't seen him since he set off for the church.

Mrs Moore That's intolerable.
Mrs Dicks It's terrifying. He could be anywhere. He could be dead.

Mrs Hurst enters

Mrs Hurst Mr Rick Dicks is outside in a taxi. He says "Thank you very
much", but he won't come in.
Mrs Dicks He what?
Mr Dicks The little toe-rag! I'll kill him!
Mr Moore Not if I get to him first.
Mrs Moore I want a word with that swine!

They all make a move towards the door R

Carla enters L. *She carries a suitcase*

Carla I should all look this way, if I were you!

Tamsin appears, now dressed in her own clothes

They all turn

Tamsin Remember me?
Carla I'll take your case out.
Tamsin Thanks, Carla. You're a mate.

Carla carries the case out R

The four parents all shout at once

Mrs Moore Case? Where are you going?
Mr Dicks What's going on?
Mr Moore I don't understand.
Mrs Dicks What's happening?
Mrs Hurst (*suddenly, loudly*) Oh, give the girl a chance to speak, do!

They look in surprise at her

(*Quieter*) Well, you should.

Tamsin Thanks, Mrs H. I'm going on my honeymoon with Rick.

The parents are dumbfounded

Mrs Moore But, but——
Tamsin Not married? But we are. We were married yesterday in a
    Registry Office.
Mr Moore But—but——
Tamsin Why today?
Mrs Moore Well, of course, "Why today?"
Tamsin We didn't want to rob you all of the pleasure of sitting together
    in that church united by selfless thoughts of our happiness. You would
    have been, wouldn't you?

Murmurs of "of course", "yes", "naturally" from the parents

    You see, Rick and I love each other, but you've been so busy disapprov-
    ing of each other that we got forgotten somewhere along the line.
Mr Moore But these people——
Mr Dicks Your mother and father——
Tamsin You see. (*To her mother and father*) You want Rick and I to be
    like you, and you (*she turns to Mr and Mrs Dicks*) want Rick and I to
    be like you. We don't want to be either, believe me. Wish us luck.
Mrs Hurst Good luck, dear.
Tamsin Thank you, Mrs H. (*To the others*) We don't hate you. We just
    don't like you very much. Sorry.

Tamsin exits R

The four parents sit down in stunned silence

The kitchen door opens and Mr and Mrs Charlton, and Mrs Peters,
enter, each carrying a cardboard box

Mr Charlton We've got the booze!
Mrs Charlton And the food!
Mrs Peters (*seeing the faces*) Is everything all right?
Mrs Hurst (*with some joy*) It couldn't be better. Let's all have a nice
    prawn vol-au-vent!

The CURTAIN *closes*

The Lights come up on Writer and Pauline. She closes the script. She is laughing, and Writer looks offended

Writer You're laughing!
Pauline I'm sorry. I thought it was funny.
Writer It wasn't supposed to be!
Pauline Well, it was.

He snatches the script and chucks it in the waste-paper basket

You're not going to throw it away?
Writer Yes, I am. I *will* write something serious and savage if it kills me. I will not be laughed at!
Pauline It's happiness, laughter. What's wrong with that?
Writer There's nothing wrong with it, but it's not important, is it? Not in the scale of things. Not in a global sense.
Pauline Oh, you're global now, are you?
Writer A funeral! They're always comedies, aren't they, funerals? Well, not mine—not the new play. It's serious and it's savage.
Pauline What happened to global?
Writer It's still there. It's an allegory—an allegory for a world tearing itself to pieces!
Pauline Oh dear.
Writer I can see it now. The curtain rises.

Stage Manager enters angrily

Stage Manager For the last time, this curtain does not rise! A hot-air balloon rises—a soufflé rises. This curtain does not!
Pauline I thought you didn't like feet.
Writer Feet?
Pauline You said if the curtain rises, the first thing you see is feet.
Writer You're right.
Stage Manager Of course she's right!
Writer The curtains open.
Stage Manager Slowly?
Writer Slowly.
Stage Manager Thank you!

Stage Manager hurries off

Writer The curtain opens slowly, to reveal——
Pauline Reveal what?
Writer Stark drama!

The Lights on Writer and Pauline fade down

The CURTAIN *opens*

The set is a working-class living-room

> *Mrs Banks, dressed in black, enters from the hallway carrying a wreath*

She looks round for an appropriate place to put it. She tries leaning it against some sherry bottles on the sideboard, and steps back to look at the effect

> *Mrs Cohen enters from the kitchen. She also wears black, but has a very gaudy pinny over it*

Mrs Cohen I don't think that's very respectful.
Mrs Banks Well, he did like his sherry.
Mrs Cohen Even so.
Mrs Banks Yes, you're probably right. I blame Edie. Trust her wreath to arrive after the funeral. (*She looks round and substitutes the wreath for a picture on the wall*) What about there?
Mrs Cohen By rights it should be at the cemetery.
Mrs Banks Well, I don't have a car. You don't have a car. How's it going to get there?
Mrs Cohen One of the others will have to run it down. I've done egg and I've done ham and I've done corned beef.
Mrs Banks You're Jewish. You're not supposed to do ham.
Mrs Cohen I'm not supposed to eat ham. There's nothing to say I can't make ham sandwiches.
Mrs Banks Well, I suppose you know your own religion.
Mrs Cohen Which is more than can be said for that lot at the funeral. They're atheists to a man—and woman.
Mrs Banks You have to pay your respects, though.
Mrs Cohen To him? To Wally? Why?
Mrs Banks Because he's dead.
Mrs Cohen So's Hitler.

Mrs 'Banks points to the wreath on the wall

Mrs Banks Don't mock respect. You were the one who said it was disrespectful to lean that against a sherry bottle.

Mrs Cohen I respect the occasion, not the person.

Mrs Banks Well, don't say anything when they come back.

Mrs Cohen Why should I say anything? I came to help with the food, not to say anything.

A radio blare is heard, approaching

Cyril?

Mrs Banks Cyril.

Mrs Cohen I'll put the jam in my sponges.

Mrs Cohen exits into the kitchen

Cyril enters. He is a young man in black motor-cycle leathers and crash-helmet. He holds a ghetto blaster to the side of the helmet

Cyril I'm here first because nobody wanted a pillion.

Mrs Banks Oh, show some respect, Cyril, do!

Cyril Why?

Mrs Banks snatches the ghetto blaster and switches it off

Mrs Banks I said "Show some respect"!

Cyril I'm in black.

Mrs Banks They're leathers.

Cyril It's the only black I've got.

Mrs Banks Well, take that helmet off, at least! That was your Uncle Wally who was buried today.

Cyril The vicar said he'd gone to a better place.

Mrs Banks Yes, well, I'm sure he has.

Cyril Mind you, anywhere would be a better place than round here, wouldn't it? (*He sits down*)

Mrs Banks You're squeaking.

Cyril I was just expressing an opinion.

Mrs Banks Those leathers. They're squeaking.

Cyril Well, they do.
Mrs Banks Not at a wake they don't. Squeaking at a wake is not
respectful. Go and change!
Cyril I don't take orders. I'm a rebel.
Mrs Banks Go and change.
Cyril Yes, Mum.

Cyril exits. The ghetto blaster blares

Mrs Banks And turn that off!

The blaring music stops

Mrs Cohen enters from the kitchen

Mrs Cohen The cars are coming.
Mrs Banks I wonder how Madge will take to being a widow.
Mrs Cohen It's not something you *take* to. It's something you get used to.
Mrs Banks Mmm. Shh! Here they come.

*The funeral party enters. This comprises Wally's widow, Madge; Mr
and Mrs Wilson; and Madge's daughter, Jackie. They all wear black*

*They find places to sit in near-silence. All that can be heard are whispered
sibilants. Nobody knows what to say. The silence is broken by a huge
sneeze from Mr Wilson. Mrs Wilson nudges him in the ribs*

Mrs Wilson George!
Mr Wilson Sorry.
Mrs Cohen How did it go off, then?
Mrs Wilson Wally's got a lovely spot. Nice view of the shrubbery.
Mrs Cohen Did you apply for it, Madge, or was he allocated it?
Madge Just allocated, I suppose.
Mr Wilson He always was lucky, Wally.
Mrs Wilson George!
Mr Wilson Well, he was.
Mrs Banks I don't think anyone could claim it's lucky to die. Sorry,
Madge.
Madge What for?

Mrs Banks Using the word. I could have said "passed over".
Madge You could have said "left over". It all means the same thing, doesn't it?

Her apparent bitterness causes an embarrassed silence

Jackie Is there anything to eat?
Mrs Banks That's up to Madge.
Jackie Is there anything to eat, Mum?
Madge (*to Mrs Banks*) I thought you and Miriam were doing sandwiches?
Mrs Cohen We have. I've done egg. I've done corned beef and I've done ham.
Mrs Banks No, I meant it's up to Madge to say when we eat. It is her do, after all.
Mr Wilson Well, I'm hungry.
Mrs Wilson George! Madge?
Madge I think we should wait for the vicar.
Jackie Oh Mum, you didn't ask *him*, did you?
Madge He more or less invited himself.
Mr Wilson How long do we have to wait, then?
Mrs Wilson As long as it takes.

Cyril enters. He has shed his leathers and is now in a T-shirt and jeans. He carries his ghetto blaster

Cyril I'm hungry.
Jackie That's what I said.
Mrs Banks We're waiting for the vicar.
Cyril Why? Is he doing the catering?
Mr Wilson (*chuckling*) Is he doing the catering?
Mrs Wilson George!
Mrs Banks Look, show some respect, do! We're here to mourn, not make pigs of ourselves.
Madge Oh, let them have something in the kitchen, if they're that hungry.

Jackie gets up

Jackie Come on, Cyril.
Cyril Right. Can we take a bottle of sherry with us?

Mrs Banks No!

Mrs Cohen And don't eat all of the same sort.

Cyril and Jackie exit into the kitchen

Madge I thought you were hungry, George.

Mr Wilson I am, Madge, but I'm not without a sense of duty. You need a man here at a time like this.

Their exchanged looks give the lie to this

Mr Stiles (*off*) Hallo? The door was open.

Mr Wilson See what I mean? (*He gets up*) Come through, vicar, do.

Mr Stiles enters. He is obviously not the vicar

Mr Wilson Oh.

Madge Hallo, Mr Stiles.

Mr Stiles Good-afternoon. Good-afternoon, everybody.

All Good-afternoon.

Mr Stiles Many, many condolences, Mrs Moore.

Madge Thank you.

Mr Stiles And can I have my tools back?

Madge Tools?

Mrs Banks At a time like this?

Mr Stiles He's borrowed masses. He's had some of them for years.

Mrs Cohen *Did* have.

Mr Stiles Did have, then. The principle's the same.

Mr Wilson I assume you can *prove* the alleged borrowing of these tools?

Mr Stiles I don't have a written document, if that's what you mean.

Madge Look, Mr Stiles. Go through to the shed and pick out what's yours.

Mr Stiles I'm obliged, Mrs Moore.

Mrs Banks I'll go with him, all the same. (Sotto voce) I don't like his eyes.

Mrs Cohen And I'll come as an umpire.

Mr Stiles It's not a cricket match. I just want my tools back.

Mr Stiles, Mrs Banks, and Mrs Cohen go off L, towards the garden

Mrs Wilson The vicar's taking his time, isn't he?

Madge I think he had another one to do after Wally.

Mrs Wilson A full life.
Madge Pardon?
Mrs Wilson For the vicar.
Madge Oh.
Mr Wilson Talking of borrowing...
Madge We weren't.
Mr Wilson Weren't we? I thought we were.
Madge No. We were talking about the vicar.
Mr Wilson Yes, but before that we were talking about borrowing.
Mrs Wilson (*catching on*) Vis-à-vis Mr Stiles.
Madge Well, he's all right. He's gone to the shed, under escort.
Mr Wilson I don't know how to put this, Madge.
Madge Put what?
Mrs Wilson Wally.
Madge Yes?
Mrs Wilson He borrowed something from us as well.
Madge Tools?
Mr Wilson Fifty pounds.
Madge *What?*
Mrs Wilson It was for your birthday. He said he wanted to buy you
something really nice.
Madge I see.
Mrs Wilson We're not asking for it back now, naturally.
Mr Wilson Though if you *did* want to get it out of the way——
Mrs Wilson When it's convenient!
Madge Yes, of course. Is that vicar coming or not?
Mr Wilson I'll hang about outside in case he misses the house. I *am*
hungry.

Mr Wilson goes off to the front door

Mrs Wilson What *did* Wally buy you for your birthday?
Madge Oh. Well, it was very nice.
Mrs Wilson Yes, but what was it?
Madge Well——

Mrs Banks and Mrs Cohen come in from the garden

Mrs Cohen You'd better come, Madge. He's going mad in that shed.

Mrs Banks He's claiming everything he lays his hand on.

Madge gets up

Madge Wally! Oh.

Mrs Wilson I'll get George. He'll have to do.

Mrs Wilson goes off R

Mrs Banks There's always Cyril.

Madge Well, it would make two, I suppose.

Mrs Banks Cyril! (*She goes to open the kitchen door. It does not open*) The door's locked.

Madge and Mrs Banks look at each other in some alarm

Mrs Cohen I'll write down everything he's taking. It could be used in evidence.

Mrs Cohen goes off L

Mrs Banks bangs on the kitchen door

Mrs Banks Cyril! Open this door!

Madge Jackie! Why's the door locked?

Jackie (*off*) It's jammed.

Cyril (*off*) That's it. It's jammed.

Madge Well, unjam it—this minute!

A little pause

> *Cyril and Jackie enter from the kitchen. Both look a little flustered.*
> *Cyril's T-shirt now has the large design on the back, and Jackie's*
> *blouse is buttoned up wrongly*

Cyril They're great sandwiches.

Mrs Banks Why did you lock the door to eat sandwiches?

Jackie We didn't. It just jammed.

Madge All on its own?

Jackie It's this house. It's all higgledy-piggledy.
Madge Like the buttons on your blouse!
Mrs Banks (*pointing at the design on Cyril's t-shirt*) And that was there!

Mrs Wilson enters

Mrs Wilson Edie's here. She's fallen off a bus.

Mr Wilson helps Edie come in. She is dishevelled and limps

That's it, Edie. Put your weight on me.
Edie Oh, Madge, I'm ever so sorry I missed Wally. I took the wrong bus.
Mrs Wilson Then she fell off it.
Edie I've been half an hour crawling up that road.
Mrs Banks We didn't see her, you see.
Mr Wilson We thought it was a Rottweiler when we first saw her. I mean, she was all hunched up—low down, you know.
Edie I'd sooner be sat down than described, thank you.
Madge Of course you would, Edie.
Mrs Wilson George! (*She wants him to help*)
Mr Wilson What?
Mrs Wilson Sit her down.
Mr Wilson Oh, yes. There you go, Edie.

Mr Wilson lowers Edie into a chair

Madge Jackie, make your cousin Edie a cup of tea.
Jackie Yes, Mum. Do you want to give me a hand, Cyril?
Cyril Right. Yes.
Mrs Banks Good boy.

Cyril and Jackie exit into the kitchen

Madge gives Mrs Banks a significant look and Mrs Banks catches on

I'll give them a hand.

Mrs Banks exits into the kitchen

Madge Now, are you all right, Edie?

Edie I think so, but I've shaken all my insides up.

Mrs Wilson I've got some smelling salts somewhere. (*She looks for the smelling salts*)

Edie I'm sorry I missed it, Madge, I really am.

Madge Missed what?

Edie The funeral.

Madge (*having forgotten it almost*) Oh.

Edie He fell off his perch, you see.

Mrs Wilson That's putting it rather crudely, Edie. Here's your smelling salts. (*She gives them to Edie*)

Edie No. Joey, my budgie. He just lay there on the bottom of his cage with his little legs sticking up in the air. I couldn't leave him, could I?

Mr Wilson Wally was a *person*, Edie.

Edie I know, but I couldn't *do* anything for Wally, could I?

Madge It's a fair point. Did Joey—you know—as well?

Edie No. It was like a miracle. I'd got his cardboard box ready and I was just writing his little epitaph when he suddenly jumped on to his little perch, rang his little bell and started to sing *Onward Christian Soldiers*.

Mr Wilson Giving thanks, I suppose, in his own little way.

Edie It's the only song he knows.

Mrs Wilson They did *Lead Kindly Light* for Wally.

Edie Did he choose it?

Madge No—he was just allocated it, I think.

Edie I'm sorry I missed it, Madge. I'll be honest—Wally and I didn't always see eye to eye, but I'm sorry I missed seeing him off.

Madge What was that big row you had about? You never did say.

Edie And Wally didn't?

Madge No.

Edie Then both our lips are sealed. I mean, I know his are anyway, but mine are by choice.

Mr Wilson It wasn't about money, was it?

The kitchen door opens

Cyril (*off*) Why not, Mum?

Mrs Banks (*off*) Because I say so! Now, take that tea out!

Cyril enters with a tray of tea-things, followed by Mrs Banks

Here we are, Edie. I've made tea for everybody. Is that all right, Madge?

Madge 'Yes, of course.

Mr Wilson I'd sooner have a sherry, personally.

Mrs Wilson You'll wait for the vicar! I'll give you a hand, Irene. (*She helps Mrs Banks pour and distribute tea*)

Jackie enters from the kitchen

Cup of tea, Jackie?

Jackie bursts into tears and exits into the kitchen

What's the matter with her?

Cyril Her life's only ruined, that's all. Mum said——

Mrs Banks Never mind what mum said!

Mrs Cohen enters L

Mrs Cohen I was promised a man half an hour ago!

Madge Oh, I forgot. George—have a word with Mr Stiles, will you?

Mr Wilson What about?

Mrs Cohen He's going mad in Wally's shed, that's what about!

Edie Why would he go mad in Wally's shed?

Mrs Wilson Tools. George—see to him.

Mr Wilson I was just going to have a cup of tea.

Mrs Wilson See to him!

Mrs Banks And you go with him, Cyril.

Cyril Look, in case anybody's interested, I'm dealing with a personal crisis.

Mrs Cohen So's Madge. She's being robbed blind out there!

Cyril A *very* personal crisis.

Mrs Banks Move!

Cyril Yes, Mum.

Mr Wilson (*moving to the exit*) Come on, Cyril—and if he makes one false move, hammer him!

Cyril But he's got the hammer!

Mr Wilson exits, and Cyril follows

Mrs Banks Come on, Miriam, we'd better make sure they don't make complete fools of themselves.

Mrs Cohen I'm beginning to hate that shed.

Mrs Banks and Mrs Cohen go off after Mr Wilson and Cyril

Mrs Wilson looks in the kitchen

Mrs Wilson She's still crying in there.
Edie Mourning for her father, I suppose.
Mrs Wilson She was cheerful enough at the funeral.
Edie Shall I talk to her? I could tell her about Joey getting back on his perch. That might cheer her up.
Madge No. I'll talk to her. If we could have a few minutes to ourselves.
Mrs Wilson Yes, you could tidy up, Edie.
Edie Right. Where's the hoover?
Mrs Wilson Yourself!
Edie Oh yes. I must look a bit of a sight.
Mrs Wilson I'll come up with you. I could do with a re-spray myself.

Mrs Wilson and Edie exit R

Madge goes to the kitchen door and opens it

Madge Jackie, come here.

Jackie enters from the kitchen

Why were you lying on the floor?
Jackie I was thinking of gassing myself, that's why!
Madge We're electric.
Jackie I'd forgotten. Oh, Mum, I'm so confused. Cyril proposed to me, but Mrs Banks said it could never be. She won't have it.
Madge I see. Did she say anything else?
Jackie She said she'd take his motor bike away if he defied her. She's got no right to say that, even if she did pay for it.
Madge Look here, I don't think Cyril is such a good idea. I mean, he doesn't have much in the way of prospects, does he?
Jackie He's got a decent job. He's a courier.
Madge Well, he won't be, if his mum takes his motorbike away.
Jackie I don't care what she does! And why are you against it?

Madge Because I am.
Jackie That's no reason.
Madge It's all the reason you're getting!
Jackie Well, you can't forbid it.
Madge Jackie, believe me—I can.
Jackie On what grounds?
Madge All right. On the grounds that——

Mr Wilson enters L

Mr Wilson He ran over my foot!
Madge Who?
Mr Wilson Him! He's a lunatic!

Mr Stiles wheels in a wheelbarrow, full of tools and paraphernalia. Mrs Cohen tries to restrain him

Mr Stiles I'm taking what's mine! And will you leave go of me, you old bat!
Jackie Where's Cyril?
Mrs Cohen This brute knocked him out!
Jackie Cyril! My Cyril!

Jackie rushes off L

Mr Stiles I did not knock him out. The fool trod on a rake. Now, if you'd all like to get out of my way...
Mr Wilson Do as he says. He's unstable!

Mrs Cohen stands in front of the barrow

Mrs Cohen You'll have to run me over first!
Madge Mr Stiles, please! Look, that can't all be yours, surely?
Mr Stiles Every last thing!

Mrs Wilson enters

Mrs Wilson Murderer!
Mr Stiles I didn't touch him!

Jackie enters with Cyril, who has his head tilted back, a blood-stained handkerchief held to his nose

Jackie Look at his poor nose! Oh, my Cyril!
Cyril Oh, my Jackie!
Madge Get him sat down.

Jackie leads Cyril towards a chair. With his head tilted back, he can't see where he's going, and steps on Mr Wilson's foot

Mr Wilson Ow! That does it—that's definitely broken now.

Mrs Banks enters R

Mrs Wilson We shall sue you through every court in the land!
Mrs Banks (*seeing Cyril*) Cyril? Who did that to my child?
Cyril He did, Mum!
Mrs Banks Oh, you did, did you?
Mrs Cohen And you called me an old bat.
Madge And I've just realised you've got a wheelbarrow in my living-room!

Mr Stiles snatches up a rake, and holds it out like a rifle with a bayonet

Mr Stiles Right, that's it! One step closer and I'll use this, so help me! (*He prepares to defend himself*)

Edie enters R *and screams loudly*

Madge Edie, what is it?
Edie (*pointing*) My wreath!

Nobody but Mrs Banks and Mrs Cohen know that it was on the wall

Why is my wreath hanging on the wall?
Mrs Banks It came late, Edie. I thought it looked quite nice there.
Edie It's an omen, that's what it is! It's my own hypocrisy staring me in the face!
Mr Stiles She's hysterical.
Mrs Wilson We know what she is. George, hit her!

Mr Wilson I've got a bad foot.
Edie Blood! There's blood on Cyril! It's an omen!

They now move away from the area around Mr Stiles

Mrs Cohen It's a nosebleed.
Edie Ahh! It's the Devil with his fork.

Vicar enters R

Vicar The door was open. I did knock, but——

Edie sees him and grabs his coat

Edie It's an angel! (*She points at Mr Stiles*) Drive the Devil out of this house!
Madge Oh, Edie, do get a grip of yourself! (*She shakes Edie from behind*)
Edie He's got hold of me!
Mrs Wilson Edie! (*She shakes Edie very hard*)
Mrs Banks Sit her down. Sit her down.
Vicar If it's an inopportune moment...

They sit Edie down. She now subsides into quieter hysterics

Mrs Cohen (*to Mr Stiles*) This is your fault, this is!
Mr Stiles I didn't hang any wreath on any wall!

Vicar notices the wreath

Vicar Surely that should be at the...
Mrs Cohen You're not connected to the wreath, but you are connected to that wheelbarrow!
Mr Stiles I'm just trying to get through this madhouse!
Mr Wilson You're the one who's mad!
Madge And get off my carpet!
Vicar Please!
Madge Get off my carpet, *please*, then.
Mr Stiles Look, one dash and I'm out of the way.
Cyril Chuck them over the wall.

Mr Stiles You try and chuck me over the wall! You just try!
Cyril Not you! The tools. Why not chuck *them* over the garden wall?
Mr Stiles Why didn't I think of that?
Jackie Because you're not Cyril!
Mr Stiles Then I'm grateful for small mercies!

Mr Stiles backs off L *with the wheelbarrow*

Madge Fool of a man! Sorry about that, vicar. We've had a bit of an afternoon here.
Mr Wilson We've had injuries!
Cyril Two.
Mrs Banks Hysterics. We've had hysterics.
Edie I just had a turn. It was seeing my wreath on the wall.
Vicar Yes, I'm still not quite sure——
Madge We've had an attempted suicide.
Jackie Only we're electric, you see.
Mrs Cohen Then, of course, we've had the madman with the wheelbarrow.
Vicar Surely these were all outpourings of grief in their own way?
Madge Grief?
Vicar For Wally?

Wally has obviously been forgotten in all this, but they are willing to accept Vicar's explanation

All Oh, Wally! Yes! Yes, of course! That's it! Wally. Grief. Yes.
Vicár May I...?
Madge Yes, of course, vicar. I think we should *all* sit down.

They all find somewhere to sit

Mr Wilson We can all have a sherry now the vicar's here. (*He moves swiftly to the sherry bottles*)
Mrs Wilson Your foot got better quickly.
Mr Wilson It's easing off.
Mrs Cohen What about my sandwiches?
Cyril No, I couldn't eat any more, thanks.
Mrs Cohen I meant everyone else! Madge?

Madge No. I think we'll let the vicar say his piece first. Help with the sherries, will you, Jackie?

Jackie does so, as do Mrs Banks and Mrs Wilson

Mrs Banks Is that everybody? What about you, Edie?
Edie No, thanks. I tend to go peculiar on sherry.

Mr Wilson raises his glass

Mr Wilson Well, good health!
Mrs Wilson George!
Mr Wilson Oh yes—sorry. Would "Cheers!" be all right?
Vicar Actually, before we imbibe, I think we should take a moment to think of dear, departed Wally.

This had not been on anybody's mind, but they do. We notice a distinct lack of love in their expressions. Vicar raises his glass

To Wally.

They raise their glasses

All To Wally.
Vicar Who is in all our thoughts today.
All Who is in all our thoughts today.
Vicar No, you don't all have to repeat that, I was simply giving voice to what I'm sure we are all feeling.
All Oh.

They all drink

Vicar I can't claim that I knew Wally well. In fact, I don't think I ever saw him in church. But, be that as it may, I sense very deeply the great affection you all hold for him.
Madge Do you really?
Vicar I do.
Madge Then you're off your chump, vicar, because no-one in this room liked him at all.

This produces a stir and shocks Vicar

It needed to be said. We've been hypocrites all day—going through the motions, that's all we've been doing—wearing our black—trying to look mournful. Mournful? I feel as happy as a sandboy, and that's the truth.
Vicar It's shock. (*To all*) It is shock, isn't it?

He gets no affirmation

Edie I said I was looking at my own hypocrisy when I looked at that wreath. I never liked Wally. He was cruel. Do you know his idea of a joke? He ate my goldfish. That's what the row was about, Madge.
Jackie He used to tease me all the time. No fun in it—just spite.
Cyril I'm glad he wasn't my father.
Madge He was, Cyril.
Cyril Mum?
Mrs Banks It *was* some time ago.
Cyril Well, obviously.
Jackie But that means that my Cyril—can't be my Cyril.
Madge That's what I was going to tell you earlier.
Jackie He's ruined my life.
Mrs Cohen He ruined mine thirty-two years ago.
Mrs Banks Miriam, not you as well?
Mrs Cohen It was fireworks night. I'm sorry, Madge, but he did have a way with him.
Madge He must have had.
Vicar Ladies, please!
Mr Wilson Just a minute, vicar—just a minute! (*To Mrs Wilson*) Gloria, have you got anything to tell me?
Mrs Wilson How dare you!
Mr Wilson Have you got anything to tell me?
Mrs Wilson He *did* have a way with him—the swine. I'm sorry, Madge.
Madge He was a busy bee, wasn't he?
Mr Wilson And I lent him fifty quid!
Mrs Wilson Well, at least he remembered Madge's birthday.
Madge He never remembered my birthday in his life, but he *was* drunk for a week.

Vicar stands up

Vicar I'm sorry. I must go. I can't cope with a situation like this. I'm not up to it. I feel totally inadequate. I'm sorry.

Vicar hurries out

Madge Good old Wally. Even when he's dead he manages to make the vicar feel inadequate.
Mrs Cohen I think we should eat my sandwiches.
Mrs Banks And take the sherry with us.

General agreement, and they all move to exit into the kitchen. Cyril puts his arm round Jackie's waist, but then they look at each other and he drops it sadly. Mrs Wilson tries to put her arm round Mr Wilson's waist, but he slaps it away

They exit

Only Edie is left as she remembers her wreath, still hanging on the wall. She takes it off the hook

Edie Nobody's taken my wreath to the cemetery. (*She looks at it for a moment*) Oh, blow you, Wally! That's where you belong! (*She drops the wreath in a waste-paper basket*)

She exits into the kitchen

Writer suddenly rushes on stage

Writer No, no, no, no, no!

Pauline enters from the kitchen

The set has now become their own home

Pauline What on earth's the matter?
Writer They did it all wrong! They made it funny!
Pauline Who did?
Writer The actors.
Pauline What actors?

Writer The actors in the play. I could kill the lot of them.
Pauline Love, there aren't any actors.
Writer But...
Pauline You must have imagined them.
Writer I must have done. Well, I'll tell you something I'll do if I ever imagine actors like that again. I shall re-cast!

Pauline moves down stage and looks out as if through windows

Pauline It's a murky evening out. Shall I draw the curtains?
Writer Yes. Draw the curtains.

CURTAIN

FURNITURE AND PROPERTY LIST

Further dressing may be added at the director's discretion

On stage: Desk. *On it:* typewriter, manuscript
Chair
Waste-paper basket. *In it:* several pieces of screwed-up paper
Another waste-paper basket
Sofa
Bottle of brandy
Sideboard. *On it:* sherry bottles
Glasses
Wall picture

Off stage: Yoghurt (**Catherine**)
Tray of tea-things (**Mrs Hurst** and **Cyril**)
Suitcase (**Carla**)
Cardboard boxes (**Mr** and **Mrs Charlton, Mrs Peters**)
Wreath (**Mrs Banks**)
Ghetto blaster (**Cyril**)
Wheelbarrow. *In it:* tools (including a rake) (**Mr Stiles**)

Personal: **Mrs Moore:** hat
Ted: business card
Cyril: blood-stained handkerchief

LIGHTING PLOT

Property fittings required: nil
2 interior settings

To open: Overall general lighting

Cue 1	**Stage Manager** exits *Fade out lights on Writer and Pauline*	(Page 2)
Cue 2	The CURTAIN closes *Bring up lights on Writer and Pauline*	(Page 18)
Cue 3	**Writer**: "Stark drama!" *Fade out lights on Writer and Pauline*	(Page 20)

EFFECTS PLOT

Cue 1   **Mr Moore**: "…kept calling me 'mate'."   (Page 12)
         Doorbell rings

Cue 2   **Mrs Dicks**: "…on my left foot!"   (Page 16)
         Doorbell rings

PRINTED IN GREAT BRITAIN BY
HOBBS THE PRINTERS LTD, SOUTHAMPTON.

Lightning Source UK Ltd.
Milton Keynes UK
UKOW06f0132071215

264243UK00001B/41/P

9 780573 121326